TRACE ELEME
ARANDA\LAS

COLUMBIA BOOKS
ON ARCHITECTURE
AND THE CITY

Columbia Books on Architecture and the City
An imprint of the Graduate School of Architecture,
Planning, and Preservation
Columbia University
1172 Amsterdam Ave
407 Avery Hall
New York, NY 10027

arch.columbia.edu/books

Distributed by Columbia University Press
cup.columbia.edu

Trace Elements

By Aranda\Lasch

Designers: Kristian Henson and Clara Lobregat Balaguer (HWGL)
Design Assistance: Patrick Slack
Copyeditor/Proofreader: Ellen Tarlin

978-1-941332-33-7

This book has been produced through the Office of the Dean,
Amale Andraos, and the Office of Publications at Columbia
University GSAPP.

Director of Publications: James Graham
Managing Editor: Jesse Connuck
Associate Editor: Isabelle Kirkham-Lewitt

Library of Congress Cataloging-in-Publication Data

Names: Aranda\Lasch (Firm), author.
Title: Trace elements / Aranda\Lasch.
Description: New York : Columbia Books on Architecture and
the City, 2017. Includes bibliographical references and index.
Identifiers: LCCN 2017016058 | ISBN 9781941332337
(pbk. : alk. paper)
Subjects: LCSH: Aranda\Lasch (Firm) | Architecture, Modern--21st
century--Themes, motives.
Classification: LCC NA737.A67 A4 2017 | DDC 724/.7--dc23
LC record available at https://lccn.loc.gov/2017016058

# ORGANIZATION AND RUIN

# ORGANIZATION AND RUIN

# ORGANIZATION AND RUIN

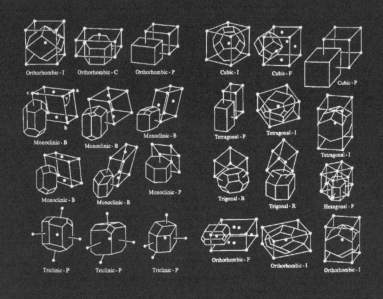

Twenty-four crystal lattice structures along with their reciprocal Wigner-Seitz cell types. The variations result from different ratios of governing lattice axes— cubic, rhombic, trigonal, so on—which thereby defines a distinct cell. Metals, snowflakes, diamonds, and salts. Crystals, like this, have highly ordered, periodic structures that repeat in all directions. This table reveals how few spatial models are actually needed to describe every known solid-state material in the universe.

Humankind has defined itself by the way it builds civilizations: the Stone Age, the Bronze Age, the Industrial Age, and the Silicon Age. By all accounts, the Silicon Age is ending and we are now entering the Nano Age. History is marked by the quest to exert control over our world, today, extending down to the molecular level. But if we've learned anything along the way it's that increased order and control is met with, in equal measure, an escalated potential for uncertainty and destruction. Control is a double-edged sword. •

Transmission electron microscope (TEM) image of GeTe crystals. Image by the Agarwal Group at the University of Pennsylvania.

The most transformative cultural acts waver on the knife's edge between coming together and falling apart. In the realm of materials, this new alchemy is referred to as self-assembly, a phenomenon that describes how, given the right conditions, molecules reorganize into new structures all by themselves. •

ORGANIZATION AND RUIN

0098  20KU      X25    1mm  WD38

Treasure Chest, Thyssen-Bornemisza Art Contemporary, 2014

Creative control is handed over to matter itself in exchange for the possibility of altering the nature of the material world. This wager radically transforms our life at the very source: the battery in your phone, the chip in your computer, the monitor you look at. These are all possible because of the reinvention of materials and the ways these materials guide energy. •

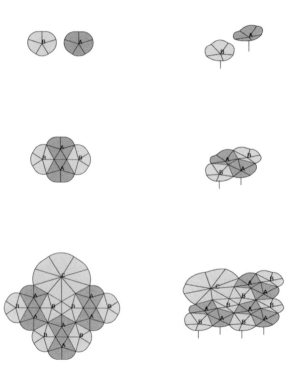

Covered Walkway, Libreville, Gabon, 2013

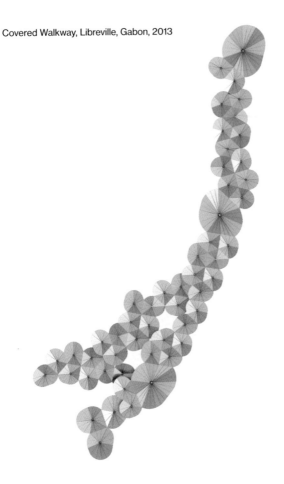

"We are moving out of the world of data classification and into the world of pattern recognition."

Marshall McLuhan, 1964

New material potentials atomize the domain of design. Everything is designable, even at the smallest scale. This motto is the basis from which our culture is transforming; it has blurred the already fuzzy edges of the discipline of architecture with daunting possibility.  •

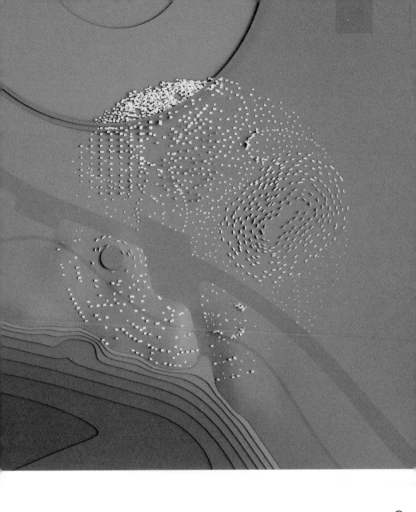

Another Circle, Columbus, OH, 2017

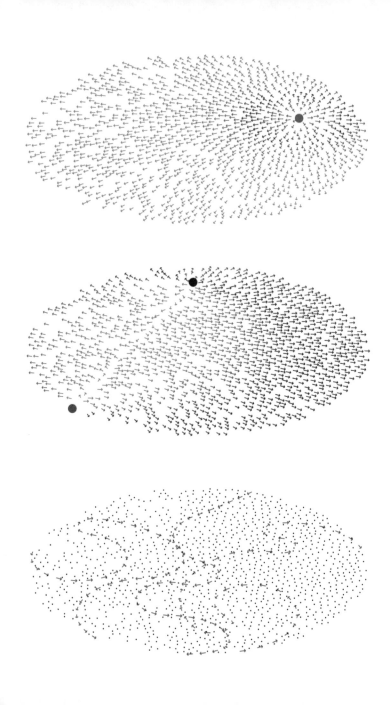

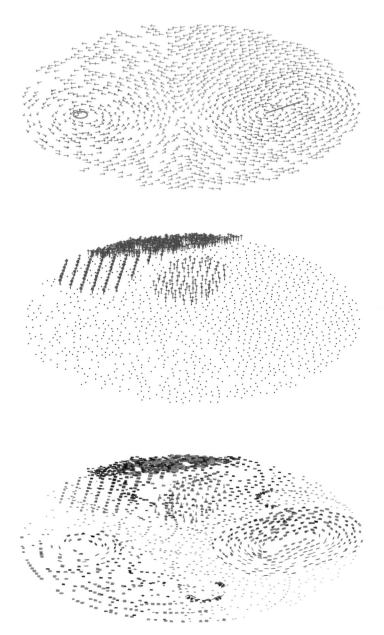

ORGANIZATION AND RUIN

Henri Labrouste, *Imaginary Reconstitution of an Ancient City*, undated. Copyright Académie d'architecture, Paris, 255.1.

Architecture, too, is an inherently destructive act. It is the physical breakdown of materials into their constituent parts, like a brick for a house or a pipe for a bathroom, standardized and recomposed into new stable structures. Architecture is a codified material system of bits and pieces intended to build and rebuild. •

Joseph Michael Gandy, Aerial cutaway
view of the Bank of England from the
south-east, 1830. Copyright Sir John
Soane's Museum, London.

Destruction with the promise of renewal.
Architecture has been here before. •

Primitive Series, Miami, FL, 2010

The greatest upheavals in industry occurred at a moment exhausted by orthodoxy and technology. This moment defined architectural culture at the end of the eighteenth century. In the midst of movement forward, many voices questioned tradition. But certain figures also remained fascinated by ruin, the soft foundation upon which to build the future. •

Grotto, New York, NY, 2005

Giovanni Battista Piranesi, *Remains of the Temple of the God Canopus at Hadrian's Villa*, Tivoli, 1748; from *Vedute di Roma* (Rome: Bouchards and Gravier, 1750).

Giovanni Battista Piranesi formed vital new structures from the fragments of previous civilizations. Assembled from fragmented sources, he conjured wild new possibilities from the rocks found in the detritus of Rome and Pompeii. These whimsical and haunting drawings of ruins reproduced and imagined new possibilities for buildings that never existed. •

Giovanni Battista Piranesi, *Via Appia and Via Ardeatina*; from *Le Antichita Romane* (Rome: Stamperia Salomoni, 1756).

"Fax machines have provided architects with that final breakthrough for what they consider to be the ideal situation and that is if they're known to be drawing they need never make their minds up."

Cedric Price

Art Deco Project, Miami, FL, 2015

Gustave Doré, *The New Zealander*, 1872;
from William Blanchard Jerrold, *London: a Pilgrimage* (London: Grant and Co, 1872).

In Gustave Doré's painting *The New Zealander*, the future is a ruin to learn from. An architect from the new world sits in the foreground, sketching the old world of London in ruin. Just as Britain was once a Roman territory and British architects drew from the ruins of Rome, now noblemen from new territories may learn from the glorious remains of London. •

20 Bridges for Central Park, New York, NY, 2011

The sarcophagus of Seti I in the dome of Sir John Soane's house; from *Illustrated London News*, 1864.

How these early studies of ruination became a system of formation, and how they helped architects, like Sir John Soane, rescue the discipline from an overbearing classicism, is a lesson that architects today can carry into the future. •

Rules of Six, MoMA, 2008

Both the ruin and the nanostructure share a ragged edge of possibility. The most dynamic work lies at the fringe of order and disequilibria. The place where matter unfolds unpredictably, caught between its own internal rules and the new ones it's introduced to. •

Henri Labrouste, *Gate and Walls of the Alatri Citadel*, 1829; from the Bibliothèque nationale de France, Paris, Prints, VZ-1030 (8) FOL.

Perceiving ordered pattern is an evolutionary habit. But to push order just beyond the faculty of recognition, to introduce ruin, is a vital exercise. It is only on this ragged edge that, if you look in the right way, you may recognize the seemingly disordered structures for new formulations of order. •

Budidesa, Bali, Indonesia, 2015

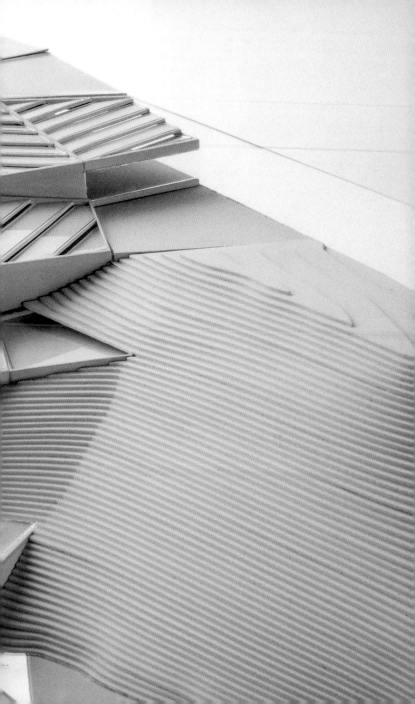

BROKEN
DRAWINGS

BROKEN
DRAWINGS

BROKEN
DRAWINGS

Railing Series, 2015

Drawings are struggles with finitude. They build from a single source that assembles with others, leaving traces, like an invisible cipher that forges lines in space. •

BROKEN DRAWINGS

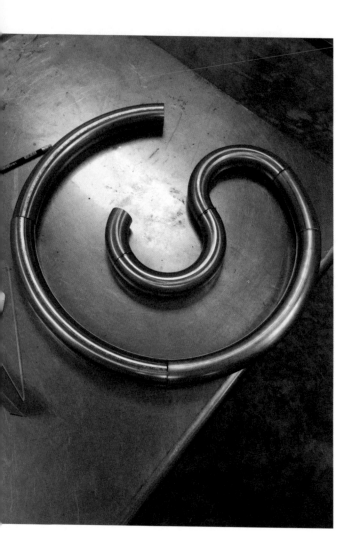

Here, the circle does not display the qualities it is most known for but rather explores what it could be. It is not whole or complete but instead grows into itself. •

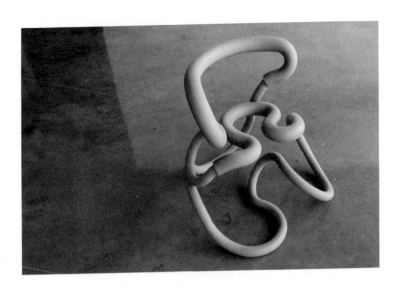

Railing Series, Gallery Diet, 2016

The source shapes, derived from simple polyhedra that shrink, grow, and attach, make three-dimensional fractals.[1] It is a drawing system that is infinitely self-scalar; modular networks expand and contract in all directions. The drawings express their underlying geometry as they carry information and gravity. •

It is a circle that refuses its own limit, a circle
that struggles to be endless. •

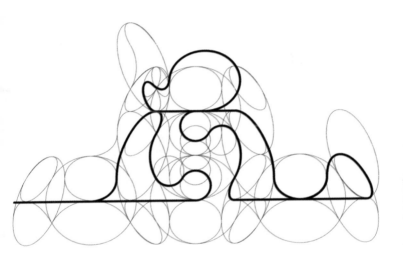

1   Fractal: coined by the French
mathematician Benoit Mandlebrot in 1975
to describe a shape more inherent to
natural pattern than classical geometry;
coming from the Latin *fractus* or "broken."
The recursive quality of fractal drawings,
self-similar parts repeating at multiple
scales, proves that complexity resides
in the part, not the whole. In other words,
the drawing is broken by itself to
make itself.

Railing: a single line that curves through a lattice of fractal circles and back onto itself to form a continuous loop. •

Night Drawing with Matthew Ritchie, Andrea Rosen Gallery, 2014

Each line is dependent on its neighbor for structure. Patterns emerge through continuity, larger assemblies yield new readings, and signals emerge from noise. •

The lines, and the drawings they make, are the structure and the space. Looping sculptures and three-dimensional drawings merge with picture language over a network of self-structural surfaces. •

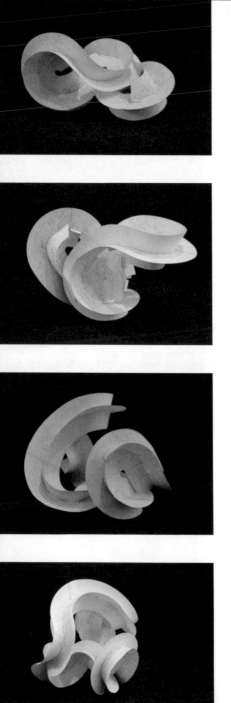

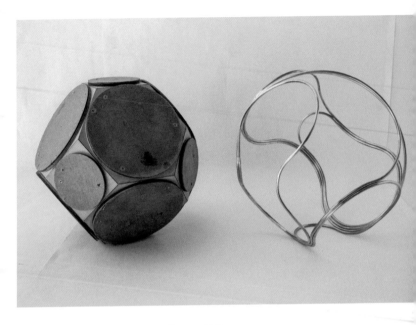

Meeting the Clouds Halfway, MOCA Tucson, 2016

They are elements in a complex layering
of work, creating continuities between
representation and three-dimensional space. •

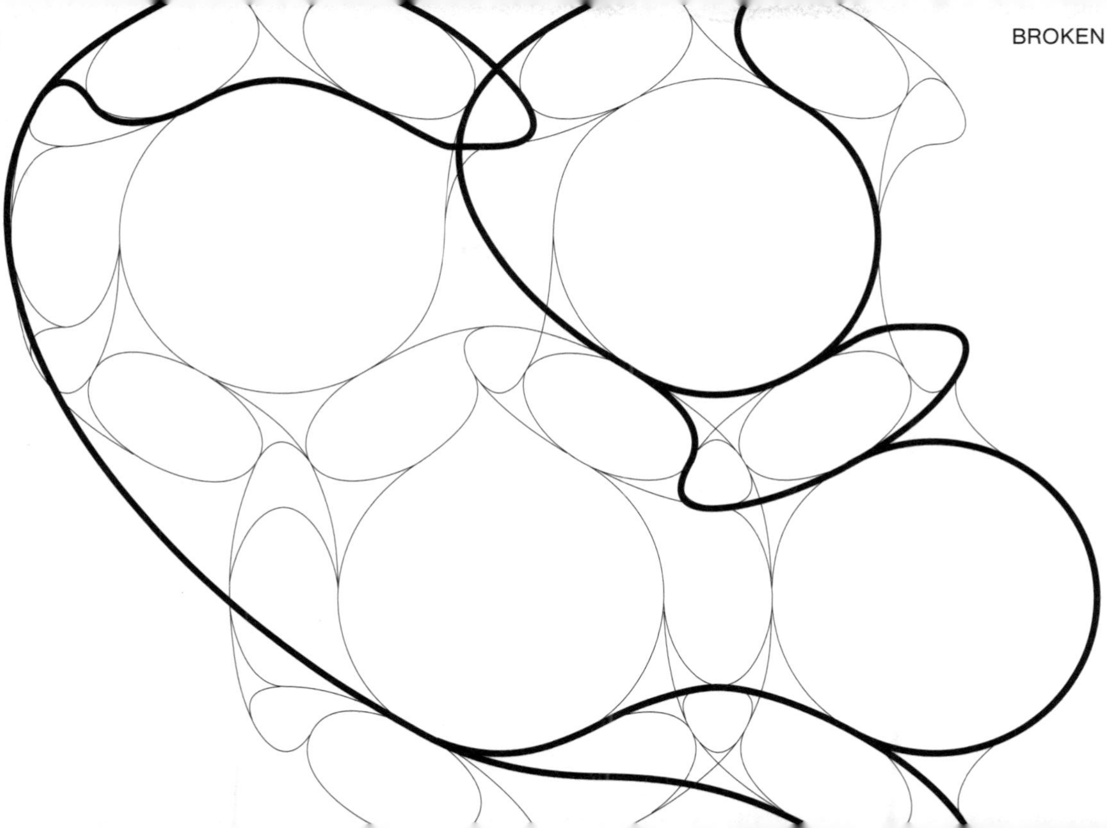

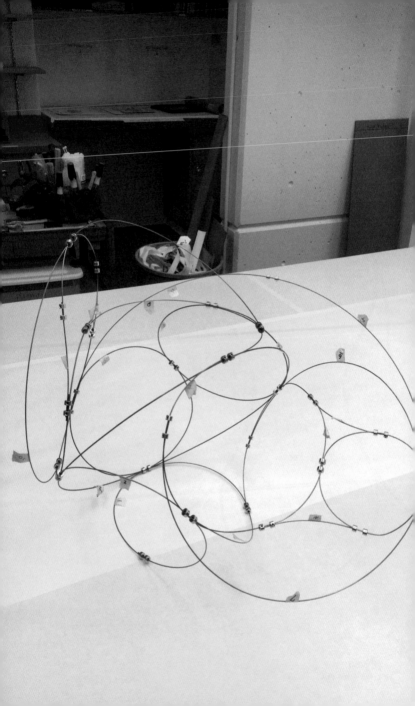

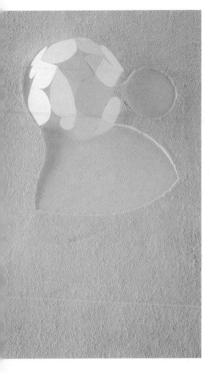

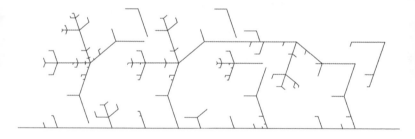

The Morning Line with Matthew Ritchie,
Thyssen-Bornemisza Art Contemporary, 2008–2013

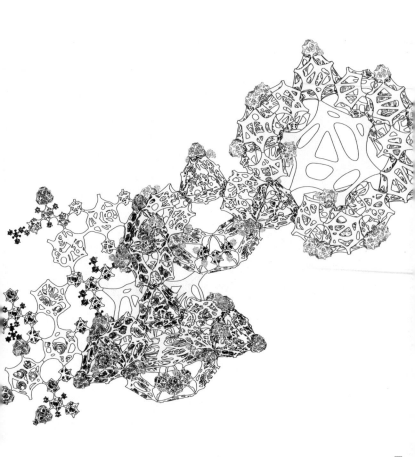

BROKEN DRAWINGS

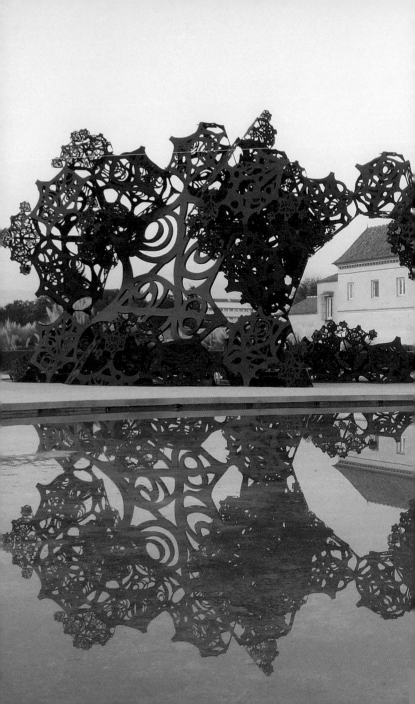

# RAGGED EDGES: THE STORY OF THE QUASICRYSTRAL

# RAGGED EDGES: THE STORY OF THE QUASICRYSTRAL

# RAGGED EDGES: THE STORY OF THE QUASICRYSTRAL

The story of quasicrystals is a strange one spanning six hundred years. It is a story marked by monsters, medieval mathematicians, higher dimensions, and extraterrestrial life. An impossible mathematical and material substance that denies our understanding of nature and yet recently found to exist within it. It is the story of the impossible becoming possible. •

RAGGED EDGES: THE STORY OF THE QUASICRYSTAL

Quasi Series, 2007

A quasicrystal is a material structure that hovers on the edge of falling apart. It is ordered but aperiodic. Unlike an ordinary crystal, whose molecular pattern is repetitive in all directions, the structural pattern of a quasicrystal never repeats itself. It is endless and uneven, described by the arrangement of modular parts. Small units aggregate to form larger figures that combine into even larger movements that are always a little bit different from the rest. •

RAGGED EDGES: THE STORY OF THE QUASICRYSTAL

Primitive Series, 2010

Quasicrystalline patterns have an infinite capacity to create and carry information. There is no end to the stories they can tell. The efficiency of modularity alongside the endless variety of pattern constitutes a step forward, or maybe a step sideways, for the discipline of architecture and design. •

The infinite is immanent in every tile or, in terms of contemporary scientific thinking, the entire universe is contained within every piece of it. What is the importance of a pattern infinitely vast, small or large? Why has it been so difficult to accept the existence of quasicrystals in the West? Why were they always deemed so impossible? In the story of quasicrystals, several significant moments and figures stand out. •

Geode Tower, 2014

**1453** A quasicrystalline motif appears in the tilework of a medieval Islamic mosque in Iran, five centuries before the pattern's underlying mathematics are understood in the West. Workers applied a special set of tiles across the surface of a building, one after the other, to create aperiodic *girih* (geometric star-and-polygon) patterns.[1]

Edge to edge, ad infinitum, these decagonal tilings form a continuous set of lines. They intuit forbidden, fivefold and tenfold, symmetries.[2] •

1    In 2007, the quasicrystalline origin of *girih* tilings was discovered by Peter Lu and Paul Steinhardt in their article "Decagonal and Quasicrystalline Tilings in Medieval Islamic Architecture," *Science* 315 (2007): 1106–1110.

2    "Forbidden" symmetries are high degree symmetries, such as five, eight, ten, or twelve-fold. Because they disallow translational periodicity, crystals that displayed these types of symmetry were, until recently, thought incapable of packing space without leaving gaps, and therefore unable to form solids.

RAGGED EDGES: THE STORY OF THE QUASICRYSTAL

Darb-i Imam Shrine in Iran, 1453. Courtesy of Peter J. Lu and Kendall Dudley. Copyright The American Association for the Advancement of Science.

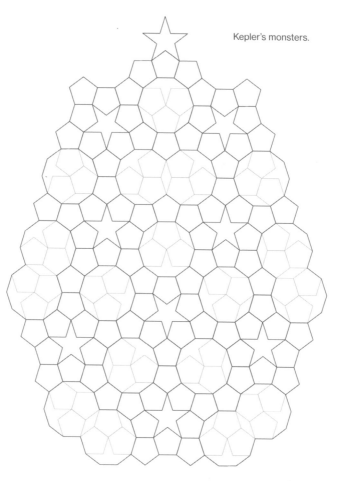

Kepler's monsters.

1619    The mathematician, astronomer, and astrologer Johannes Kepler takes up the challenge of tiling with forbidden symmetries in his book *Harmonice Mundi*.[3] When asked if he succeeded in tiling the plane with five-sided shapes, Kepler ominously affirms that he has but that he has also found "monsters" in the resulting order. Monsters: pairs of fused decagons and stars. The unexpected shapes that repeat aperiodically. Kepler was the first to witness this strange behavior, the first recorded instance of monsters in the West. •

3    Kepler's seventeenth-century treatise *Harmonice Mundi (Harmony of the World)*, published in 1619, explores the concept of congruence across geometric form, musical harmony, and the cosmos. In Book II, Kepler experiments with the symmetry of polyhedra and the orderly arrangement of pentagon tilings.

1974    Roger Penrose
          decomposes Kepler's four tilings—pentagons, pentagrams, decagons, and fused decagons—into a single pair of shapes that tile the plane aperiodically: stars, boats, diamonds, kites, darts, and rhombs. The Penrose pattern proves mathematically that aperiodic tilings exist, at least in theory—always changing. He effectively proves that a quasicrystal may exist ten years before it is actually found in nature. •

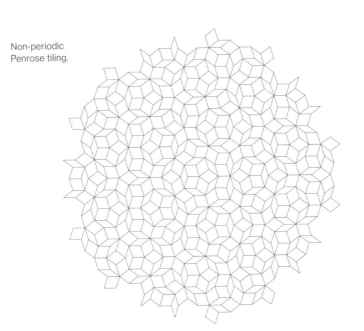

Non-periodic
Penrose tiling.

1980   Nicolaas Govert de Bruijn
       creates an algorithm that
turns Penrose's tilings into a rule.[4]
The projection algorithm is a near-
perfect description of aperiodic
order; its only problem (and not just
for architecture) is an existential
one. While it explains

4   Nicolaas Govert de Bruijn, "Algebraic Theory of Penrose's Non-Periodic Tilings of the Plane," *Proceedings*, vol. 84 (Eindhoven, NL: Eindhoven University of Technology, 1981).

quite reliably how a
crystal like this might
form, the algorithm
uses projection from a higher
dimension down to more familiar
three-dimensional space. What
we see then is actually a hyper-
dimensional object. Only its shadow
exists here in our reality. How de
Bruijn made the conceptual leap
from higher dimensions to our own
to find the algorithm of projection
has never been fully explained,
but his method remains a bridge to
another reality and back. •

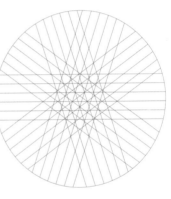

Diagram of Govert de
Bruijn's algorithm.

Quasiscreen, Las Vegas, NV, 2014

Meeting at the National Institute of
Standards and Technology (NIST) in 1985
just months after shaking the foundations
of materials science; Dan Shechtman
(left) discusses the material's surprising
atomic structure with collaborators.
Photograph by H. Mark Helfer, NIST.

Electron diffraction pattern from an
icosahedral quasicrystal showing
fivefold symmetry. Image by
Dan Shechtman.

1982    The material scientist Dan
        Shechtman discovers a
new type of synthetic solid-state
matter: the icosahedral phase.
Looking at a rapidly cooled alloy of
aluminum and manganese ($Al_6Mn$)
through an electron microscope
and using X-ray diffraction studies,
Shechtman observes an atomic
structure with fivefold rotational
symmetry. He proves that aperiodic
and non-repeating crystals do exist,
however fleeting. But Shechtman's
discovery of this crystal structure is
met with skepticism by the science
community. It is not until 2011 that
he is awarded the Nobel Prize in
Chemistry for "the discovery
of quasicrystals." •

Event Space, Miami, FL, 2015

**1984**  Two years later, Dov Levine and Paul Steinhardt coin the term "quasicrystal."[5] By identifying the symmetries and parameters that define aperiodic arrangements in three dimensions, the scientists prove that a solid analogy exists for Roger Penrose's two-dimensional aperiodic tiling—confirming Shectman's observation from 1982. The search for the physical manifestation of this mathematically true concept ends. Skeptics will still contend that while the quasicrystal is a synthetic state of matter, it does not occur naturally. •

5   Dov Levine and Paul Steinhardt, "Quasicrystals: A New Class of Ordered Structures," *Physical Review Letters*, vol. 53, no. 26 (December 1984).

Scanning electron microscope image of facetted $Al_6Li_3Cu$ quasicrystal grown from the liquid alloy. The fivefold symmetry of the facets reflects the underlying atomic-scale icosahedral symmetry. Courtesy of Frank Gayle.

RAGGED EDGES: THE STORY OF THE QUASICRYSTAL

2009   According to the scientific
          community at large,
quasicrystals still do not occur
naturally. That is until scientist
Luca Bindi reports the first natural
occurrence in a fragment of
Khatyrka. The decade-long search,
beginning in 1999 by researchers
at Princeton University, culminates
in Bindi's examination of the
"khatyrkite" mineral found in the
Koryak mountains in far-eastern
Siberia, Russia. Steinhardt and
Bindi establish that the mineral
is dated to the formation of the
solar system, delivered to earth
by meteor. The latest episode
in this winding story places the
impossible crystal at the beginning
of it all—not only possible but also
extraterrestrial. •

Ancient meteorite showing naturally
formed quasicrystals. Photograph by
Luca Bindi. Courtesy of Paul Steinhardt.

# HISTORY IS GENERATIVE

# HISTORY IS GENERATIVE

# HISTORY IS GENERATIVE

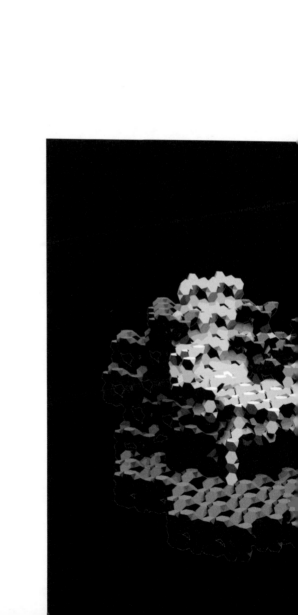

Like a material or system that is dynamic, history itself is generative. It is active with properties that shape and transform concepts. By using historical objects, or moments in history, these concepts reach back and move forward at once, like hitching a ride. •

Louis XV died in 1774. This same year, the trace element manganese is discovered. What emerges when these two histories collide? The fauteuil chair and the super-crystal structure of manganese rebuild a moment in history. •

Ore containing manganese, $_{25}$Mn.

Louis XV Fauteuil, 1774; from Frederick Litchfield, *Illustrated History of Furniture: From the Earliest to the Present Time* (London: Truslove and Shirley, 1892).

1774 Fauteuil, 2007

The Grotto: a dual obsession with boulders and eighteenth-century romantic landscapes. How to replicate this artificial cave, to siphon all the lost enchantments of the era trapped in this picturesque landscape device, is a historical and technical challenge. Can Victorian romanticism exist in modular boulders? •

Antoine Joseph Dezallier d'Argenville, Arboreal Stone and Florentine Stones, 1755; from Jurgis Baltrusaitis, *Aberrations: An Essay on the Legend of Forms* (Cambridge, MA: MIT Press, 1989).

Grotto, New York, NY, 2006

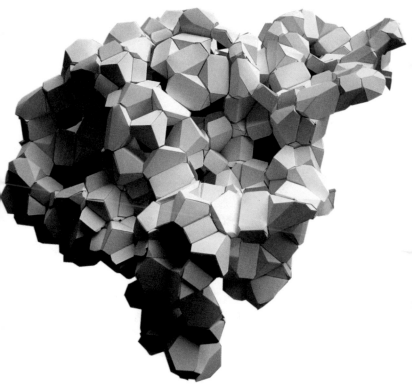

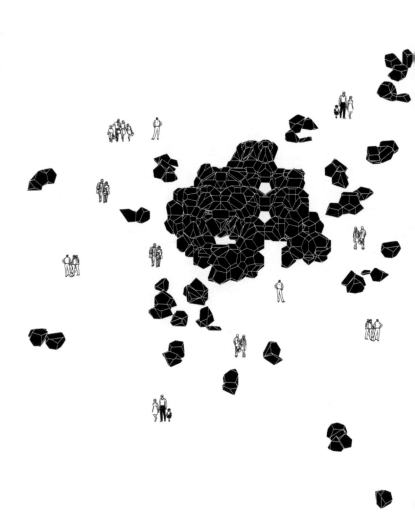

Or if a project is not an actual moment in history, maybe it is about certain inspiring figures. Wilson "Snowflake" Bentley: a farmer from Vermont and pioneer in "photomicrography" who proved with a simple homemade camera that no two snowflakes are alike. Bentley photographed over six thousand specimens across his lifetime, standing in the cold, patiently waiting for snowflakes to fall. He died of pneumonia for this crusade. •

Plate XIX of Bentley's "Studies among the Snow Crystals;" from the *Monthly Weather Review*, 1902.

Wilson A. Bentley photographing snow crystals, 1925. Courtesy of the Jericho Historical Society.

Rules of Six, 2008

An ode to Bentley, who once asked, "What Magic is there in the rule of six that makes the snowflake conform so rigidly to it laws?" His story is a contemporary one. It is about the search for an underlying cause for why matter forms in all its particular ways. •

Dating back to the ninth century, the *Subak* is a collective water management system that shapes Bali's landscape of rice paddies. The *Subak* organizes and nurtures. It breaks the hillside down into terraces, which can be irrigated and cultivated individually, but also connects to form a larger network or ecology of fields. An art foundation sited within this unique terrain is organized similarly. The units, which extend from the existing agricultural landscape, seamlessly connect art gardens and exhibition spaces into a continuous interior and exterior circuit. •

Islet in the terraced rice field of Bali, Indonesia (8°30' S, 115°26' E). Copyright Yann Arthus–Bertrand.

Budidesa, Bali, Indonesia, 2015

A new building lives in the past. Take, for example, Miami's historic architecture defined by the Art Deco movement from the 1920s to the 1940s. Bold geometric motifs shape the city's landmarks. But with a textured, pleated, concrete ripple, the city's era of decadence and ornament, is imagined with an alternate rhythm and control. •

Art Deco façade detail of the Wiltern Theater. Courtesy of Cheryl Spelts.

Art Deco Project, Miami, FL, 2015

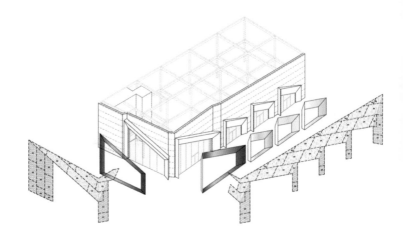

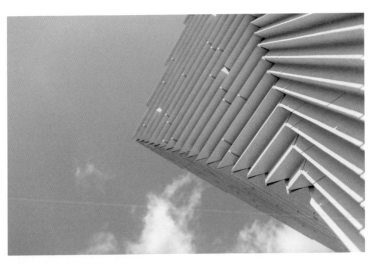

HISTORY IS GENERATIVE

HISTORY IS GENERATIVE

The ruins of a theater are revived under the shelter of a new canopy in Gabon, West Africa. The canopy emerges from a single element: an extruded aluminum and local hardwood panel. Each panel interlocks with another in a reciprocal pattern—producing a thin self-supporting structure and skin in which column and roof emerge from the same language. Over the remains of an old theater, a new one is created. •

Original Palais des Spectacles, Libreville, Gabon.

Palais des Arts, Libreville, Gabon, 2013

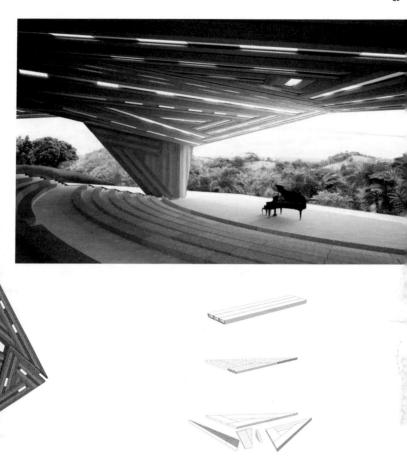

In a traditional Balinese house, each room is a separate and distinct building. In a Chinese courtyard house, each room is arranged symmetrically around a courtyard creating a connected rooftop. How might a single-family house synthesize these two domestic vernaculars? The Bali House organizes independent buildings under a continuous roof. •

Traditional Balinese house compound.

Historical *Siheyuan*, also known as a Chinese courtyard house.

Bali House, Bali, Indonesia, 2015

# BASKETS AND ARCHITECTURE

BASKETS AND ARCHITECTURE

BASKETS AND ARCHITECTURE

V

Baskets highlight the role of human ritual. A work of architecture grows from an underlay of codes, systems, and processes, building up its own concepts and logics. •

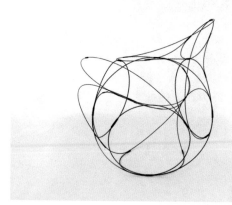

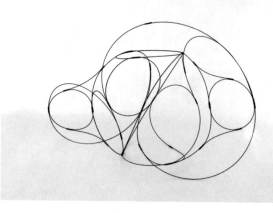

Meeting the Clouds Halfway, MOCA Tucson, 2016

Tohono O'odham Man in the
Maze basket.[1]

1    In the baskets of the Tohono O'odham tribe, ritualistic making is embodied by the coil. The act of coiling begins with a central point around which a material is wound, spiraling outward and upward in concentric circles to create a structural surface. Coiling generates form through pattern—an algorithm—building on a set of principles that can be manipulated to generate shape. Surface extends to create a plate, a bowl, a vase, or a more elaborate form. Coiling is a structural strategy for producing functional objects, but it is also a ritual for connecting the weaver to his or her community, elders, and surrounding desert environment. Ritual material culture and everyday utilitarian material culture are inseparable. Through the making of everyday objects, people reiterate the foundational values of their society. The gathering, preparation, and manipulation of natural materials into a basket guides the weaver toward understanding the world around them and their place within it. As with the O'odham peoples, cosmology is expressed through the very language of basketry. Coiling coalesces the material, spiritual, aesthetic worlds. Take I'itoi or the Man in the Maze: the creator who first brought people to earth from the underworld. The story of I'itoi tells the story of every human's uncertain journey through the labyrinth of life—a labyrinth traced by coiling and believed to be the floor plan of I'itoi's house atop Baboquivari Mountain.

Papago basketmaker, Arizona, 1916.
Courtesy of National Archives
(111-SC-202199).

In a craft like weaving, ritual and material action are always intertwined. From the foraging and preparation of a material to its transformation by hand, the weaver reiterates the foundational meanings of society. Its place in the natural world—its traditions, myths, and memories—exists in an extended process of materialization. •

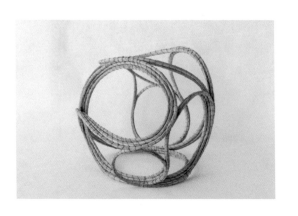

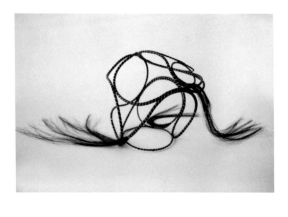

Architecture as a material practice is similarly intertwined. Embedded with larger collective structures—structures that are rebuilt and revitalized over and over again. In architecture and in weaving, there exists a disengagement from the object being formed. In both practices, the process is more about the relations around that object than the object itself. •

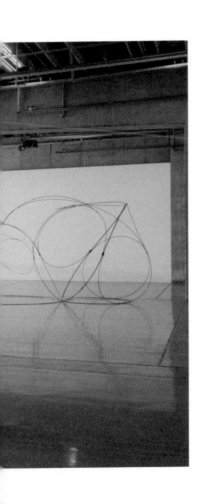

BASKETS AND ARCHITECTURE

Basket making is as much a procedural process, warp and weft, as it is a social process. It brings people together, not only those that gather to weave but also the ancestors whose tradition they continue. Native American weavers, like the Tohono O'odham tribe, speak of an object's many voices—as if each basket is in essence a conversation. •

"Many times I dream a design and it
haunts me until I actually weave it."

Terrol Dew Johnson

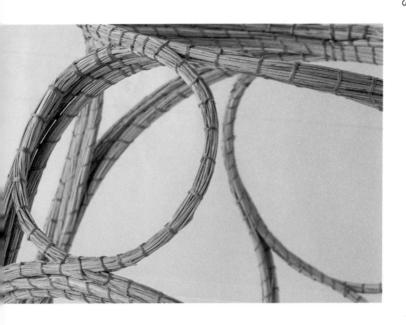

BASKETS AND ARCHITECTURE

Architecture, too, converses—between themes of universal significance, geometry and matter, and the actual experience and material through which these become manifest. It is a boundless and inspiring conversation. It reminds us that design mediates two worlds: one entirely abstract and coded, and the other very real and alive—like what we find through our interactions every day with people, communities, and cities. •

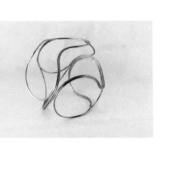

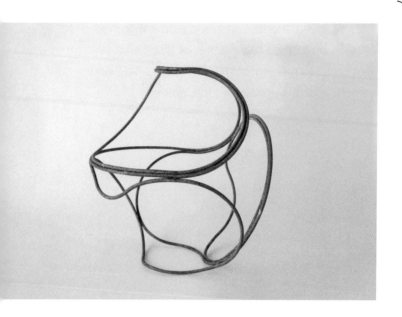

BASKETS AND ARCHITECTURE

In the end, the truly inspired moment comes with the realization that neither of these worlds is of our own making; both were always here and somehow discovered along the way. •

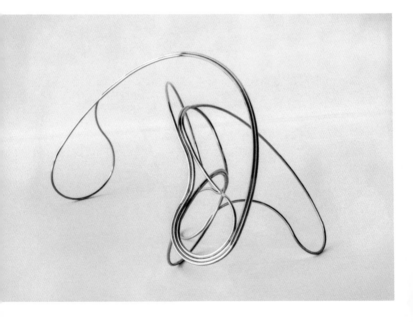

BASKETS AND ARCHITECTURE

## 215.1–7
## ANOTHER CIRCLE

Another Circle is a new public space for Mill Race Park in Columbus, Indiana, to mark the inaugural Exhibit Columbus event. The project consists of 1,800 pieces of salvaged limestone, organized to create a large three-acre field of activity. This rough circle contains a diffuse programming of spaces for outdoor recreation; a loose gathering of function inside a scattering of stone. The limestone pieces, salvaged from a local mill in Bloomington, called Bybee Stone, are then placed, stacked, and arrayed to create a theater, a beach, a riverfront, and areas for games and relaxation.

LOCATION: Columbus, Ohio
YEAR: 2017
CLIENT: Exhibit Columbus
TEAM: Bybee Stone

215.6

215.7

215.1

## 320.1–10
## QUASI SERIES

The Quasi series is about the pursuit of orders, rigorously modular but wild—on the verge of disorder. Quasicrystals, a new phase of matter discovered in 1982, represent this kind of material structure that hovers on the edge of falling apart. Unlike a regular crystal, whose molecular pattern is periodic, or repetitive in all directions, the distinctive quality of a quasicrystal is that its structural pattern never repeats the same way twice. It is endless and uneven, but interestingly, it can be described by the arrangement of a small set of modular parts. The Quasi series explores this aperiodic assembly in wood furniture. Taking the form of tables, consoles, cabinets, and other household items, the pieces are constructed from hundreds of individual walnut blocks.

YEAR: 2007–ongoing
TEAM: Johnson Trading Gallery

## 312.1–3
## FAUTEUIL

In the year 1774, Louis XV died, marking the sunset of one of history's most lavish monarchies. In the same year, a young Swede named Johann Gahn, working in the deepest and wettest levels of a mine, discovered the metal manganese. At a molecular level, manganese displays a striking "super-crystal" modularity. In this solid aluminum chair, two historic events—the super-excess of Louis XV and the super-crystal of

in your arms. The informality implicit in an ordering system is more important than expressing its strict composure. Multiple pursuits come together here—the quasicrystal, the fractal, the single building element, the landscape object—to make something atomized, frayed, and open.

LOCATION: Venice, Italy; Miami, Florida
YEAR: 2010–2014
TEAM: Fendi, Thyssen-Bornemisza Art Contemporary; IPC, The Design School at ASU

320.5

320.6

340.1

320.7

340.2

320.8

340.3

340.4

340.5

340.6

manganese—are fused into a single moment of design.

YEAR: 2007
TEAM: Johnson Trading Gallery

320.9

320.10

### 340.1–6
### PRIMITIVE SERIES

The Primitive series combines the romantic tradition of ruined landscapes with modular fractals. First realized in the 2010 Venice Biennale, it is comprised of loosely dispersed furniture elements, or "rock piles"—each unique but formed from the same universal building block. Like microcosms in the distance, the clusters are imagined as islands falling apart and building back up, organizing and eroding at once. The Primitive arrangements can be sat on, leaned against, held

215.2

320.1

320.2

320.3

320.4

215.3

312.1

312.2

312.3

215.4

215.5

## 3601–8
## RAILING SERIES

Railing is an exploration of structural modular loops that are upholstered to become furniture. Each piece of furniture is a single loop made up of many circles. Here, the circle does not display the qualities it is most known for, but it is what a circle can be. It is not whole or complete but is instead growing into itself. It is a circle that refuses its own dimension and finitude, that struggles to be endless. The Railing collection continues the studio's research into modularity through a novel language of arcs. This system allows all distinct pieces to be created from the same set of modular stainless-steel pipe arcs with upholstery in a variety of colors and materials.

YEAR: 2015–ongoing
TEAM: Gallery Diet, Gallery ALL, Nina Johnson

360.1

360.6

360.7

## 3821–4
## GEODE TOWER

The Geode Tower is a large sculptural lighting object. Built as an assembly of identical modular units, its reflective surface continually dissolves and reappears as it reacts

360.8

382.3

382.4

## 4621
## TREASURE CHEST

The Treasure Chest was commissioned by Thyssen-Bornemisza Art Contemporary for the exhibition *Treasure of Lima: A Buried Exhibition*, curated by Nadim Samman. The exhibition features the work of over thirty renowned artists, which are housed within the Treasure Chest. The chest, comprised of a spherical glass pressure vessel nestled within a faceted stainless-steel exterior shell, is intended to exhibit the work when open and to protect the work

## 5101–2
## RULES OF SIX

Rules of Six is an installation commissioned for the *Design and the Elastic Mind* exhibition at the Museum of Modern Art in New York, curated by Paola Antonelli. In collaboration with material scientist Matthew Scullin, the project explores the notion of self-assembly—where top-down methods for determining form are replaced by bottom-up rules of formation and where new material structures are not carved or composed by conventional tools but are "grown" through simple interactions between components or molecules. At the heart of the project is a custom programming environment that simulates formation over time in the same way molecules assemble themselves in the lab. This application was used to produce a large-scale wall relief mounted in the gallery alongside two monitors: one running the simulation "live" and the other displaying a slide show of actual nanostructures designed by Scullin and his colleagues. Like the nanostructures it emulates, Rules of Six is designed to multiply indefinitely without sacrificing stability. It is indifferent

510.2

## 5121–4
## GROTTO

Grotto recreates the romantic device of the Victorian garden. As an artificial structure or excavation made to resemble a cave, the grotto's structural unit is the boulder. The project thus set out to develop a set of modular boulders that when combined defy a conventional sense of order. The result is a combination of four expanded-polystyrene boulders that fit together using an underlying aperiodic logic and produce a wildly ordered three-dimensional pattern that never repeats the same way twice. As was common with grottos in eighteenth-century English gardens, there is always a hidden fountain to discover within this project. A new foam grotto that is similarly elaborate, artificial, and intimate.

LOCATION: New York, New York

to light emitted from its mirrored cavities. Programmed illuminated patterns are transmitted and distorted across the network, as the light reflects to create infinite spatial configurations. The project builds on a pair of collaborative projects with the artist Casey Reas—Primitives (This Could Be an Extraordinary Find) and the 2012 stage design for Yeasayer—which evoke the atmosphere of a research station or communications hub.

YEAR: 2014

when closed. It is designed from an imagined moment of finding hidden treasure and is buried in a secret location on the Isla del Coco. A duplicate Treasure Chest exists, which contains an encrypted map that, if deciphered, reveals the location of the treasure. The map was auctioned to raise funds and awareness for oceanic research.

LOCATION: Isla del Coco, Costa Rica
YEAR: 2014
CLIENT: Thyssen-Bornemisza Art Contemporary

to scale. Its sprawling construction could represent molecules, rooms, buildings or entire neighborhoods. The title, Rules of Six, is an ode to Wilson Bentley, the Vermont farmer who, around the turn of the twentieth century, photographed thousands of snowflakes on his homemade camera to empirically prove that no two were alike. "What magic is there in the rule of six that compels the snowflake to conform so rigidly to its laws?" Bentley wrote in Technical World, 1910. The unyielding sameness and infinite possibility that inspired Bentley to search for the hidden still inspires us to this day.

LOCATION: New York, New York
YEAR: 2008
CLIENT: MoMA

YEAR: 2006
CLIENT: PS1/MoMA
TEAM: Daniel Bosia, Arup AGU

512.1

512.2

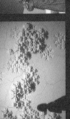

512.3

510.1

462.1

382.1

382.2

360.2

360.3

360.4

360.5

513.23

513.24

513.25

513.26

513.5

513.15

513.16

513.17

513.18

513.7

513.8

513.9

513.10

513.1

513.2

512.4

LOCATION: Tucson, Arizona
YEAR: 2016
CLIENT: Museum of Contemporary
Arts Tucson
TEAM: Curated by Alexandra
Cunningham Cameron
SUPPORT: Graham Foundation
for Advanced Studies in the Fine
Arts, University of Arizona, CAPLA,
Tohono Oodham
Community College

513.1-34
MEETING THE CLOUDS
HALFWAY

Meeting the Clouds Halfway at
the Museum of Contemporary Art
Tucson presents a series of weaving
experiments in collaboration with
Tohono O'odham fiber artist Terrol
Dew Johnson. What began as a
conversation about the similarities
of traditional Native American craft
and cutting-edge design became a
decade-long exchange to reimagine
an ancient material practice within
the needs of a contemporary world.

Coiling is at the core of the pieces
in this project, which use materials
and rituals born from the Sonoran
Desert. For many generations,
the Tohono O'odham have coiled
baskets out of desert fibers not
only for domestic use but also as a
ceremonial meditation that unites
art with life. The act of coiling

creates form through an intuitive geometric system and iterative movements. Rooted in this shared foundation of pattern-making, the collaboration produced a collection of experimental baskets and woven constructions that engaged the traditional art of basket weaving with new techniques that resulted in baskets made in a variety of materials including grass, wood, glass, concrete, plastic, and metal. The baskets were first displayed at Artists Space in New York in 2006. Ten years later works from that show were acquired as part of the permanent collection at the Museum of Modern Art. The exhibition at MOCA Tucson, curated by Alexandra Cunningham Cameron, continues the dialogue in a range of constructions, from baskets to architecture, which ultimately suggest cross-cultural sharing as a means of evolving both tradition and technology.

513.27

513.28

513.29

513.30

513.19

513.20

513.21

513.22

513.11

513.12

513.13

513.14

513.3

513.4

513.5

513.6

Istanbul to Vienna, constantly adapting its form to its new site. It is currently in the permanent collection of the ZKM in Karlsruhe Germany.

LOCATION: Seville, Spain; Istanbul, Turkey; Vienna, Austria; Karlsruhe, Germany
YEAR: 2008–2013
CLIENT: Thyssen-Bornemisza Art Contemporary
TEAM: Matthew Ritchie and Arup AGU

513.31

513.32

532.1

513.33

532.2

534.3

## 5501–2
## 20 BRIDGES

20 Bridges for Central Park is a proposition to extend the legacy of Central Park's brick, stone, and cast-iron bridges. Originally realized by Frederick Law Olmsted and Calvert Vaux, the bridges were built to connect landscapes and intertwine the park's series of footpaths, carriageways, and bridle paths. Recognized as a radical invention in landscape design at the time, they allowed for the traffic and flow of people and nature over, under, and through them. 20 Bridges connects separate landscapes in the park with a family of radically new structures—built from a single fractal unit that follows a simple trajectory in space. Whether they bridge over a small stream or a large crosstown throughway, connect land to water or shore to island, the structures explore new possibilities for inhabitation. Some are conventional footbridges; others are more unexpected, like stepping-stones over a creek or ladders up a hill. Like the original bridges, these structures highlight the essential role of Central Park itself: connecting people, places, and nature.

532.7

534.4

532.8

### 534.1–10
### NIGHT DRAWING

Night Drawing is a looping sculpture and three-dimensional drawing derived from a double Mobius strip. It is a collaboration between with Matthew Ritchie as part of his show Ten Possible Links at the Andrea Rosen Gallery, exhibited among paintings, wall drawings, sounds, and moving images. The sculpture, a merging of Ritchie's drawings over its looping surfaces, is constructed from laser-cut aluminum sheets, producing dynamic qualities that are both tectonic and self-structural.

513.34

534.5

534.6

## 532.1–8
## THE MORNING LINE

The Morning Line was conceived as a platform to explore the interplay of art, architecture, cosmology, and music. Imagined as a ruin from the future, the Morning Line is a drawing in space—each line connects to other lines to form a network of intertwining figures and narratives with no single beginning or end. Within the drawing, other information layers animate the structure. The piece is outfitted with a sophisticated arrangement of speakers and controls designed by Tony Myatt of the Music Research Centre of York University, which transform it into a spatialized sound environment. Guest composers were invited to produce site-specific works for each installation, treating visitors to music and sound performances that move through the space. The structure grows from a fractal building block that scales to produce the lines, spaces, and structure of the piece. Each block is interchangeable, demountable, portable, and recyclable—allowing the piece to change and adapt physically over time along with its sonic content. To date, the Morning Line has traveled from Seville to

Night Drawing can be thought of as one element in a complex layering of works, creating continuities from the walls into three-dimensional space.

LOCATION: New York, New York
YEAR: 2014
CLIENT: Andrea Rosen Gallery
TEAM: Matthew Ritchie

LOCATION: New York, New York
YEAR: 2011
CLIENT: Jumeirah Essex House

532.3

532.4

532.5

532.6

550.1

534.1

534.2

550.2

534.7

534.8

534.9

534.10

## 635.1
## EVENT SPACE

The Design District Event Space is a multifunctional five thousand square-foot space intended to host the neighborhood's events. Perched above the surrounding buildings with a commanding view of the district, the space is defined by two cantilevered slabs between which all the functional elements are sandwiched. The slabs are formed into a decorative relief mold, a nod to the tropical modernism in Miami's historic architecture. A custom system of folding Merbau hardwood doors retract completely to create a seamless outdoor environment that is only possible in Miami. All together, the building's bold structure, floral patterning, and airy openness produce a uniquely Floridian environment.

LOCATION: Miami, Florida
YEAR: 2015
CLIENT: Miami Design District
TEAM: Speirs + Major, SB Architects, CHM Structural Engineers

636.1

636.2

636.3

LOCATION: Miami, Florida
YEAR: 2015
CLIENT: Miami Design District
TEAM: Speirs + Major, SB Architects, CHM Structural Engineers

way, descending into a heavily forested valley along the Ayun River bank. A walking path through the art gardens and exhibition spaces creates an experience of art seamlessly integrated with nature—nature marked by large-scale contemporary art from renowned artists such as Zhang Huan, Ai Weiwei, Anselm Kiefer, Maurizio Cattelan, Adel Abdessemed, and Mona Hatoum. The museum is experienced as a landscape. The roof, which creates a sculpture park on the outside, filters light into the interior through a series of skylights. At night, Budidesa comes alive with outdoor video, projections, and reflections across the gardens to illuminate the tropical splendor of Bali in new ways.

LOCATION: Bali, Indonesia
YEAR: 2015
CLIENT: Budi Tek

## 642.B1–6
## BALI HOUSE

This residence for an art foundation is designed into a field of rice paddies in a traditional Balinese agricultural landscape. The owner, who is both Indonesian and Chinese, started the foundation as a way to promote dialogue, understanding, and exchange between the two countries. The residence, too, bridges these two worlds and combines two domestic vernaculars. In a traditional Balinese compound, each room is a separate small building arranged dynamically across the site. In a traditional Chinese courtyard house, rooms are adjacent to one another and arranged symmetrically around a communal courtyard. The combination of these two vernaculars results in a building with a continuous roofscape over independent rooms that adapts to both the local environment and the owner's own cultural background.

LOCATION: Bali, Indonesia
YEAR: 2015
CLIENT: Budi Tek

642.B4

642.B5

642.B6

## 651.1–7
## PALAIS DE ARTS

The Palais des Arts is a multifaceted performance venue in the capital of Libreville, Gabon. Its defining feature is a new outdoor theater with a large-scale canopy built in

642.A1

6511

the footprint of the old Palais des Spectacles theater. The canopy creates a new plaza—a public space sheltered from the sun and rain. The structural system proposed for the canopy is a novel prefabricated aluminum extrusion, assembled on site as a kit-of-parts. Each component consists of a "stress skin" panel in which the top and bottom surfaces contribute to the strength and stiffness of the structure. Each panel interlocks with another in a reciprocal pattern—producing a thin self-supporting structure where column and roof emerge from the same language.

LOCATION: Libreville, Gabon
YEAR: 2013
CLIENT: Agence Nationale des Grands Travaux (ANGT)
TEAM: Westlake Reed Leskosky, AKT II, Arup Lighting.

6351

636.4

636.5

642.A2

642.A3

642.A4

642.A5

642.B1

642.B2

642.B3

## 636.1–5
## ART DECO PROJECT

Art Deco is the inspiration for a new commercial building in Miami. Located in Miami's new Design District, the building houses four luxury retailers. Miami's historic architecture was shaped by the Art Deco movement from the 1920s to the 1940s—where bold geometric motifs define the city's landmarks. Inspired by the pleated Art Deco patterns found in architecture and fashion, the building façade is textured to revive the exuberance and ornament of Miami's "golden era." The façade is made from molded GFRC panels that fan out above the building's street-level retail spaces to create angular recessed storefront coffers. Lighting integrated into the panel joints creates a scattered, fleeting pattern across the façade at night.

## 642.A1–5
## BUDIDESA ART PARK

Budidesa is an art park by the Yuz Foundation in Bali. The park consists of a series of art gardens, exhibition spaces, and a residence that together form a unique combination of contemporary art in a tropical environment. The site—located just north of Denpasar, the capital of Bali—is characterized by its steep topography, framed by rice fields at the top and a river at the bottom. The surrounding rice paddies are terraced in a traditional Balinese

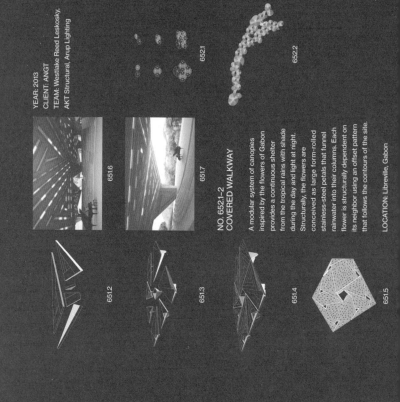

YEAR: 2013
CLIENT: ANGT
TEAM: Westlake Reed Leskosky,
AKT Structural, Arup Lighting

6521

6522

6516

6517

651.2

651.3

651.4

651.5

## NO. 6521-2
## COVERED WALKWAY

A modular system of canopies
inspired by the flowers of Gabon
provides a continuous shelter
from the tropical rains with shade
during the day and light at night.
Structurally, the flowers are
conceived as large form-rolled
stainless-steel petals that funnel
rainwater into their columns. Each
flower is structurally dependent on
its neighbor using an offset pattern
that follows the contours of the site.

LOCATION: Libreville, Gabon